You Can Play The Ukulele

BY DON BALL

WITH COMPLETE INSTRUCTIONS AND TWENTY-ONE SONG FAVORITES

CONTENTS

Associated Music Publishers, Inc.

DISTRIBUTED BY

HAL•LEONARD®

7777 W. BLUEMOUND RD. P.O. BOX 13819 MILWAUKEE, WI 53213

YOU CAN PLAY THE UKULELE!

The title tells the story: You can play the Ukulele! There's nothing tricky, tough or complicated about it. If you can whistle, hum or sing a tune — and are willing to spe a little time getting acquainted with the simple instructions and illustrations contained in this book — you'll find yourself playing the uke, and enjoying it!

You'll be amused to learn that the word "ukulele" means "flea," believe it or nct. It comes from two Hawaiian words "uku" (insect) and "lele" (to leap) and is so-called from the movement of the fingers in playing the instrument. Another thing that may surprise you: The uke is not a native of the Hawaiian Islands. It's a small guitar of Portuguese origin which was first introduced into the islands by music loving missionaries, some say around 1877. Shortly thereafter it "migrated" to America where it reproduced rapidly! Today, thanks largely to radio and television promotion by that rambunctious red-head, Arthur Godfrey, the uke is more popular than ever!

Each exercise in this book has been carefully designed to teach you chord combinations and sequences which, in themselves, are tuneful and fun to learn. And, having them, you'll be able to accompany yourself in hundreds of familiar songs.

First, study the "Get Acquainted" chart on Page three. It shows you the different parts of your uke and tells you what they're all about.

Second, take time to tune-up properly (Page four). A symphony orchesta does it: Why shouldn't you?

PRACTICE (STILL) MAKES PERFECT!

Don't be in a hurry. Practice and learn each chord exercise carefully before you go on to the next. If you do, by the time you get to "Chord Tricks" at the back of the book you'll be ready and eager to try your hand (both of 'em, in fact!) at learning to play melody.

Now — let's take a good look at the "Get Acquainted" chart.

Don Ball

THE UKULELE

This is a "Get Acquainted" chart.

It's purpose is to familiarize you with the names and locations of the different parts of your uke. Better study 'em carefully: They'll come in handy as we go along.

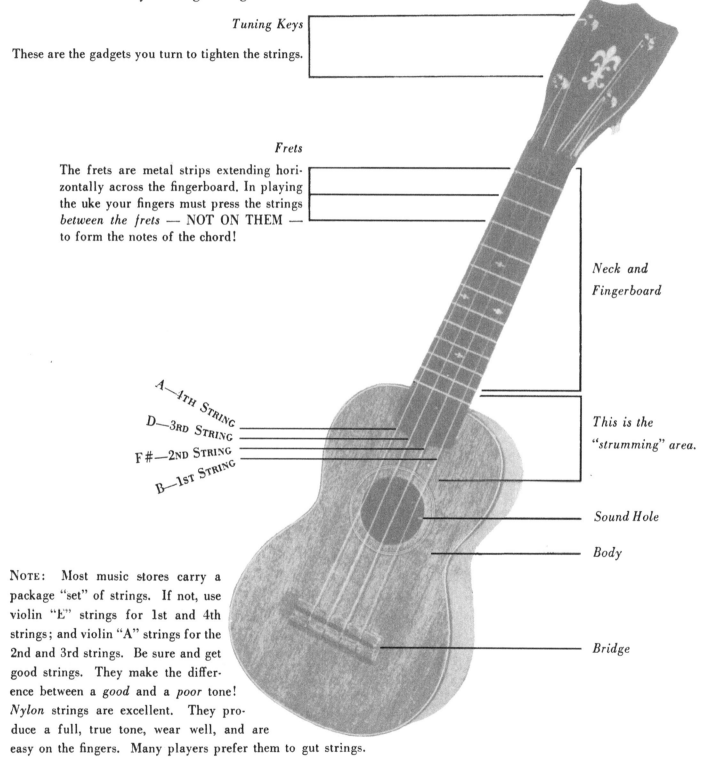

Tuning Keys

These are the gadgets you turn to tighten the strings.

Frets

The frets are metal strips extending horizontally across the fingerboard. In playing the uke your fingers must press the strings *between the frets* — NOT ON THEM — to form the notes of the chord!

Neck and Fingerboard

A—4TH STRING
D—3RD STRING
F#—2ND STRING
B—1ST STRING

This is the "strumming" area.

Sound Hole

Body

Bridge

NOTE: Most music stores carry a package "set" of strings. If not, use violin "E" strings for 1st and 4th strings; and violin "A" strings for the 2nd and 3rd strings. Be sure and get good strings. They make the difference between a *good* and a *poor* tone! *Nylon* strings are excellent. They produce a full, true tone, wear well, and are easy on the fingers. Many players prefer them to gut strings.

The instrument you own will influence to a great extent the quality of tone you will produce. For it is apparent that a better quality instrument will give you a richer, more full-bodied tone. With ukuleles, as with everything else, quality is important. Well, now that you know the "Get Acquainted Chart," let's get on with the important business of TUNING your uke.

TUNING THE UKULELE

The diagram below will show you the simplest way to tune your uke: The 4th string is tuned to the "A" above middle "C" on the piano — and the 3rd, 2nd, and 1st strings are tuned as indicated.

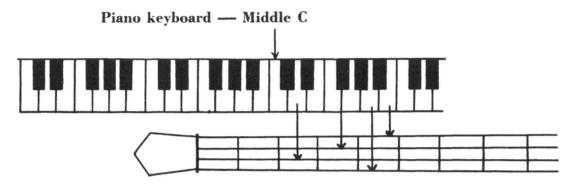

Piano keyboard — Middle C

Now, just in case you've misplaced your piano — there's another method of tuning your uke. And it's almost as easy as falling off a surf-board!

This second method involves tuning the uke *BY EAR* — a good trick, and you can do it! The diagrams below show you how in four easy steps. Reading from left to right:

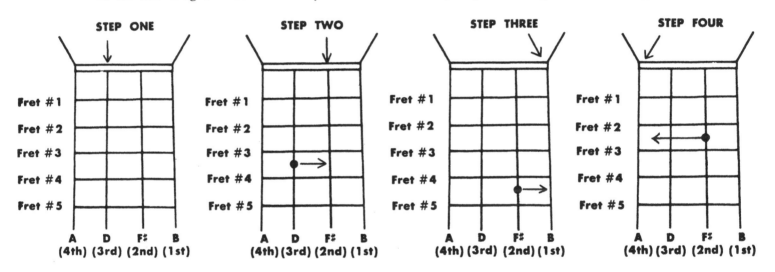

STEP ONE: Turn tuning key to tighten D (3rd) string until it gives a clear tone when you strike it. By humming the *first note* of "My Country T'is of Thee" and then *tuning the D string to this note*, you can "pitch" the uke to your natural singing range.

STEP TWO: Press your left index finger firmly on the D (3rd) string between the 3rd and 4th frets — then tune the F# (2nd) string up to this note;

STEP THREE: Again, press your left index finger firmly on the F# (2nd) string between the 4th and 5th frets — then tune the B (1st) string up to this note;

STEP FOUR: Once more, press that left index finger on the F# (2nd) string between the 2nd and 3rd frets — then tune the A (4th) string up to this note. That does it: You're in tune — and so is your uke!

Take time to tune up carefully. Follow instructions step-by-step. *Be sure of each step before going on to the next.* A properly tuned uke is half the battle — and be thankful you're not learning to play a harp!

Now let's find out how to *hold* the uke.

HOLDING THE UKULELE

There's really nothing to it!

All you do is study the picture below and follow these simple instructions:

1. Press the uke against your body with the middle of the right forearm; and —

2. Hold the neck of the uke between the thumb and fore-finger of your left hand, with the thumb supporting the neck near the first fret. Your left arm should be held well forward, with the fingertips directly over and above the fingerboard . . .

LIKE THIS

Now that you've got the situation well in hand, you're ready for the next step: Playing the uke.

PLAYING THE UKULELE

There are two ways of playing the uke: With a felt pick — and with your fingers.

USING A PICK

Hold the pick lightly but firmly between your thumb and first finger and strum gently up and down the strings just above the sound hole (see "Get Acquainted Chart," page three). Keep your wrist relaxed. Don't be in a hurry. Go Slowly at first and gradually increase your speed ("tempo" or "beat", if you prefer) until you're getting a smooth, even tone. With a little practice you'll find it easy as poi (!)

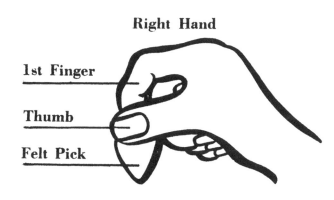

Right Hand

1st Finger

Thumb

Felt Pick

USING THE FINGERS

Start with the index finger at first. Keep it fairly limp. Use the back of the fingernail for the DOWN-stroke and the ball, or cushion, of the finger for the UP-stroke. As in using a pick, your wrist should be relaxed and "loose" — your forearm holding the uke firmly against your body. Practice this stroke until you can do it smoothly.

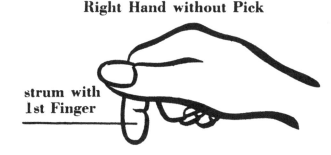

Right Hand without Pick

strum with
1st Finger

THE "ROLL" STROKE

This is a basically simple stroke which you can use with great effectiveness. It consists of three easy, separate movements which, with a little practice, you will combine into a continuous "one-two-three" roll effect.

ONE—stroke the strings DOWN-ward with the ball of your thumb; *TWO*—bring the ball of your index finger UP-ward across the strings; *THREE*—stroke DOWN-ward across the strings with the nail of your index finger. This completes the first "one-two-three" movement of the Roll stroke. Now repeat, *ONE*—DOWN-ward with the ball of your thumb; *TWO*—UP-ward with the ball of your index finger, etc. By counting "one-two-three" and using a rotating motion of your wrist, you'll find that you can master the fundamentals of this stroke with a little practice. It's a "showy" piece of business — and a lot of fun as well.

If your fingers seem clumsy and stiff at first (and they probably will) — think nothing of it! With a little practice you'll be surprised at how quickly they'll begin to limber up. Keep that wrist relaxed! Remember — easy does it.

HOW TO READ CHORD DIAGRAMS

It is standard equipment for most of us to have four fingers on each hand. For sweet *clarity's* sake, in the diagrams which follow the fingers of the *left hand* are numbered 1, 2, 3, 4 — starting with the *index finger*. The black dots on the diagrams show you *where* to put your fingers on the strings and fingerboard; the numerals indicate *which* fingers to use. All diagrams have been designed to give you the best practical and convenient fingering for each chord. They are based upon some twenty years of personal experience in playing the uke — and, to coin a phrase, "Experience is the best teacher!"

Left Hand Fingers

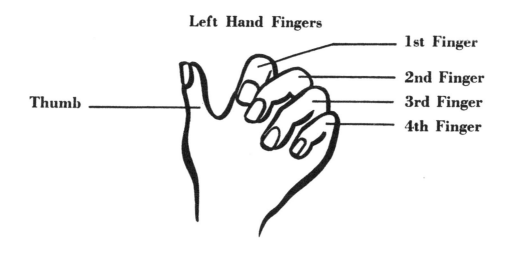

A string without a dot is an "open" string and is *not* to be fingered (pressed down) in making the chord. For example, in the diagram below the A (4th) string is an "open" string — but *all four strings must be played* to sound the chord.

A curved line connecting two or more strings (see diagram below) means that *one* finger is to be used in pressing all the strings so connected. Here the 2nd finger is used as a bar to press down firmly *all four strings* — with the 3rd finger pressing down the B (1st) string to complete the chord.

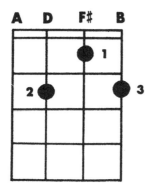

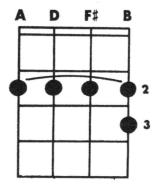

By keeping these simple instructions clearly in mind — you should have no trouble in finding and fingering the chords shown in the following diagrams. Take your time. Remember, haste makes — dischords! So, study the chord patterns carefully, practice them faithfully, and you will make progress ac-*chord*-ingly.

Exercise No. 1—Chord combinations in Key of D

D is a good *beginning* key: The three basic chords — D, G, and A 7th (see diagrams below) are easy to learn, and will enable you to accompany a good many familiar songs.

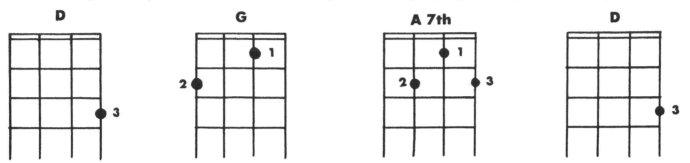

Practice these chords until you can change positions quickly and easily. Then go on to the next group below.

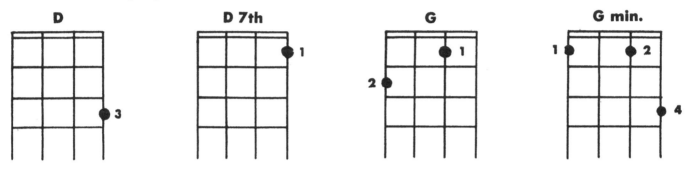

Two new chords were added: D 7th and G *minor.* Practice *this* sequence in order, reading from left to right D, D 7th, G, G min. and returning to D to finish.

This next group of chords contains a pair of minor chords — B min. and E min. — frequently used in the key of D. Also F# 7th — one of the best and busiest chords on the uke. Practice *these* in sequence, too.

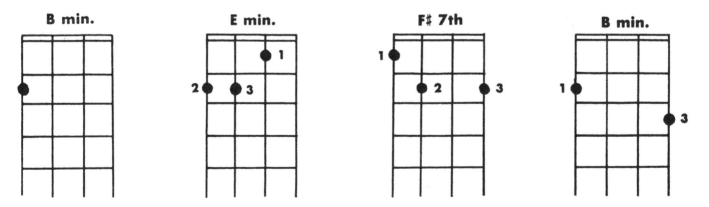

Practice all of these chords until you know what each one sounds, feels, and looks like! Then try out these two chord sequences and discover what a happy combination they make:

1. D, D 7th, G, G min., D, A 7th, and D

2. D, F# 7th, B min., E min., F# 7th, and B min.

After you've mastered these two combinations, try working out some of your own.

My Bonnie Lies Over The Ocean

Excercise song–Key of D

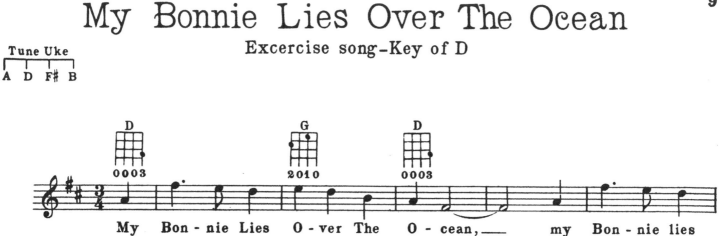

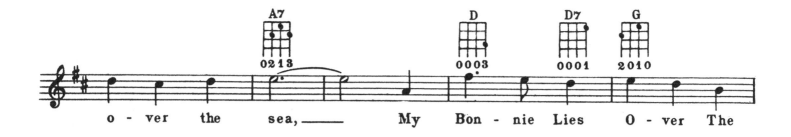

My Bon - nie Lies O - ver The O - cean,____ my Bon - nie lies

o - ver the sea,____ My Bon - nie Lies O - ver The

O - cean,____ oh bring back my Bon - nie to me.____

Bring back, bring back, oh bring back my Bon - nie to me, to me.

Bring back, bring back, oh bring back my Bon - nie to me.____

Exercise No. 2—Chord combinations in Key of G

G is a logical "next step" in these exercises — and a very useful key. Again, let's start with the basic chords — G, C, D 7th, back to G.

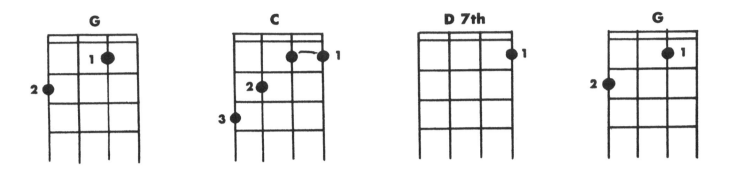

As with the first exercise in key of D, practice these basic chords in order shown until you can change positions easily and naturally. Then on to the group below.

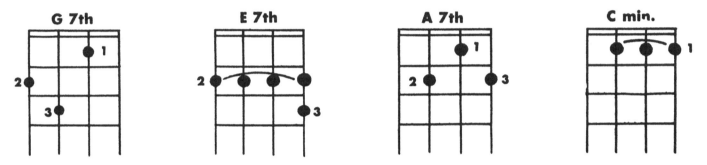

You'll find the G 7th and E 7th chords, very useful; also the C minor. For a pretty chord sequence, try playing this combination: G, G 7th, C, C min., G, D 7th, and back to G to finish.

In the group below, A min. and B 7th will be new to you. Practice the chord sequence from left to right as shown below.

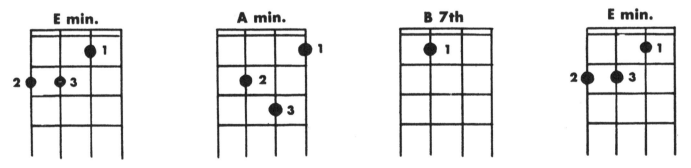

As you did with Exercise No. 1—practice all these chords, individually and in the combinations indicated, until you get the "feel" of them and can play them easily and cleanly.

Once you've learned the chords in *just the two keys of D and G,* you,ll discover that there are literally *dozens* of familiar songs you can accompany yourself on.

And, by the way, are you trying out those strokes you were working on back on page six?

Auld Lang Syne

Exercise song- Key of G

Exercise No. 3—Chord combinations in Key of A

As in the two previous exercises, we start out with the three basic chords — the "work horse" chords — in this key: A, D, E 7th, and back to A.

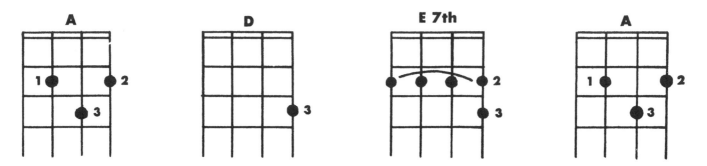

The only chord new to you in the group below is D minor. Try playing A 7th, F# 7th, B 7th, D min. and back to A. Now, for variety, play this combination: A, A 7th, D, D min., A, E 7th, and A.

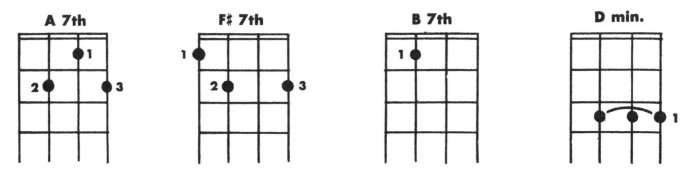

In the group below, two new chords have been added — F# minor and C# 7th. Practice them in connection with your old friend B minor. Play in order from left to right across the page as in previous exercises.

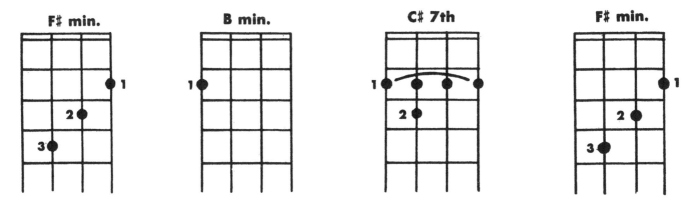

As a good chord-and-finger exercise, try the following chord combinations: A, C# 7th, B 7th, E 7th, and back to the A position. The only really tricky chord in this entire exercise is C# 7th—but with a little practice you'll soon have it eating out of your hand!

Go back and review exercises 1 and 2 and notice how many chords you learned there have carried over into this exercise.

Now let's go to "C" — in the next exercise!

Old Folks At Home

Exercise song–Key of A

By STEPHEN FOSTER

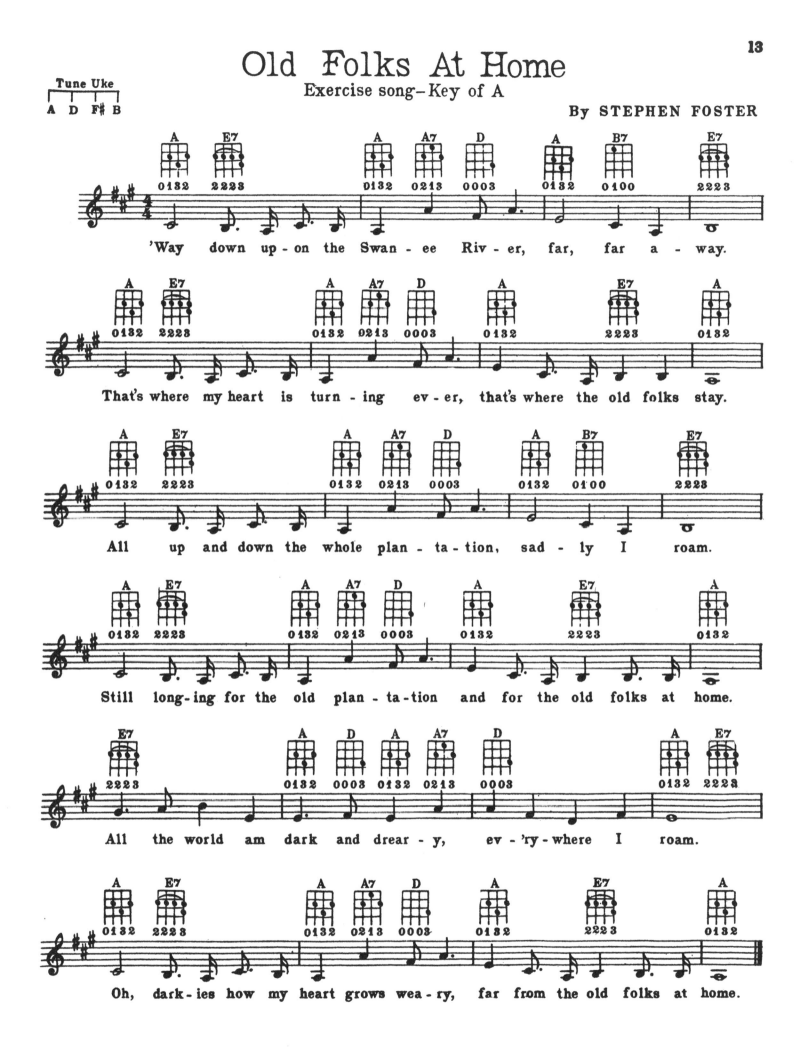

Exercise No. 4—Chord combinations in Key of C

Once more, let's begin by learning the three basic chords in C. They are: C (surprise!) F, G 7th. Play in order shown.

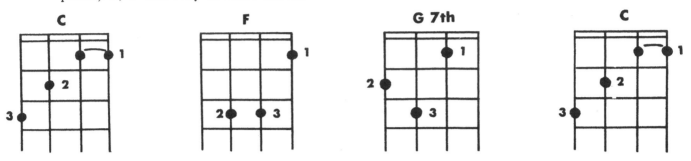

In the chords below something *really* new has been added: A second position for the F and G 7th chords. Practice them carefully. Try changing from F to F (2nd position) and from G 7th to G 7th (2nd position).

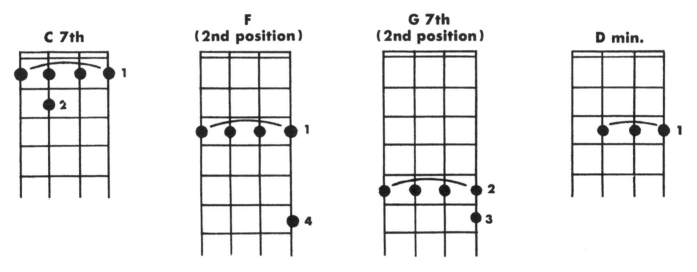

F minor is the only new chord in the group below. You'll find the fingering a bit tricky at first, but practice it until your 3rd and 4th fingers go where they should! Try playing C, C 7th, F, F min., C, G 7th, and C.

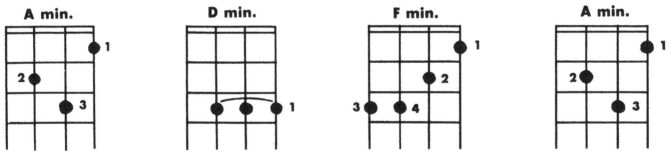

After playing the minor chords above — refer to Exercise No. 3 and borrow the E 7th chord for *this* combination: A min., D min., E 7th, and A min.

The chord combinations in the four keys you've been studying — D, G, A, and C — will enable you to play accompaniments to any number of familiar songs, old and new. The following pages take you a few "fancy steps" further by illustrating some advanced chord positions and techniques.

Annie Laurie

Exercise song- Key of C

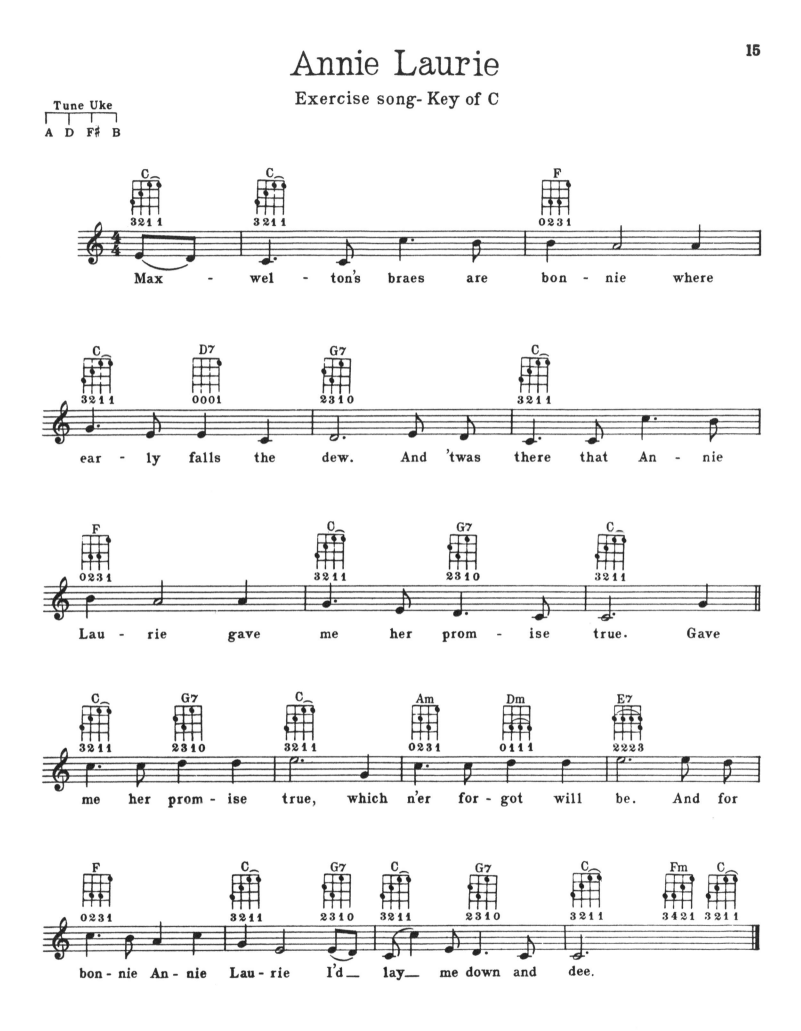

DIMINISHED SEVENTHS

These are handy chords to have around—invaluable aids to "barbershop" harmony!
Also, once you've educated your fingers to form the 2nd chord in the progression (see
Position 2, below) the rest is easy: All you do is move *the same chord formation* up the
fingerboard, fret by fret — obviously nothing for you to fret over!

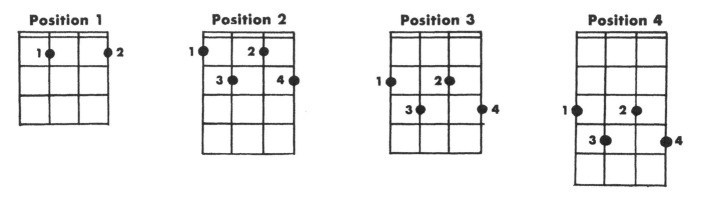

Position 1 **Position 2** **Position 3** **Position 4**

The chord progression below illustrates a practical use of the diminished seventh
chord in a typical chord sequence. This combination can be used as a "vamp" or intro-
duction to a song in the key of G.

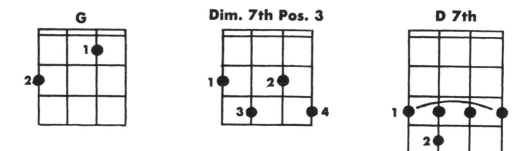

G **Dim. 7th Pos. 3** **D 7th**

For a big finish to any song you may play in the key of A — practice the chords below.

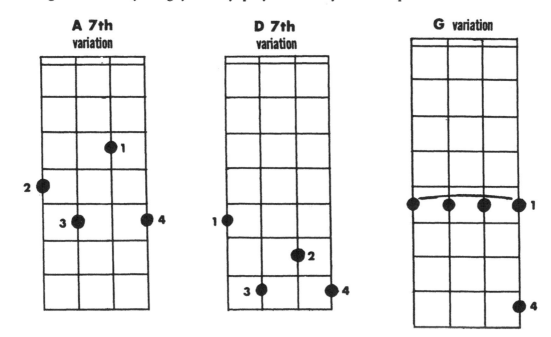

A 7th
variation

D 7th
variation

G variation

MINOR CONSIDERATIONS

Here, all on one page for review and ready reference, are the *Minor* chords- you'll need from to time. Some of 'em you've already met.

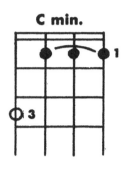

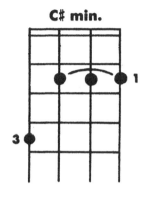

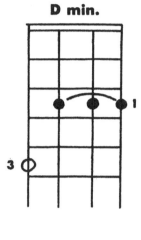

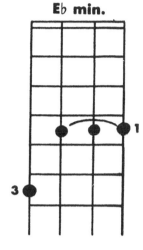

Where open-faced dot appears it indicates optional fingering.

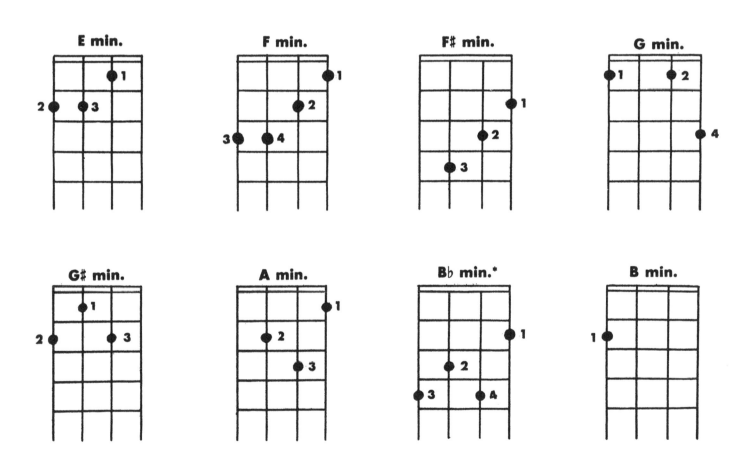

* The fingering here is a little involved. If you get it the very first time you have accomplished a "minor" miracle!

"LUCKY SEVENTHS!"

Some of these Seventh chords you know already. For convenience sake *all* of the 12 necessary chords are given below.

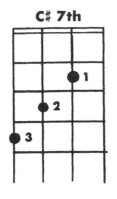

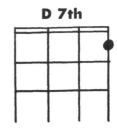

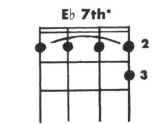

Don't be in a hurry.

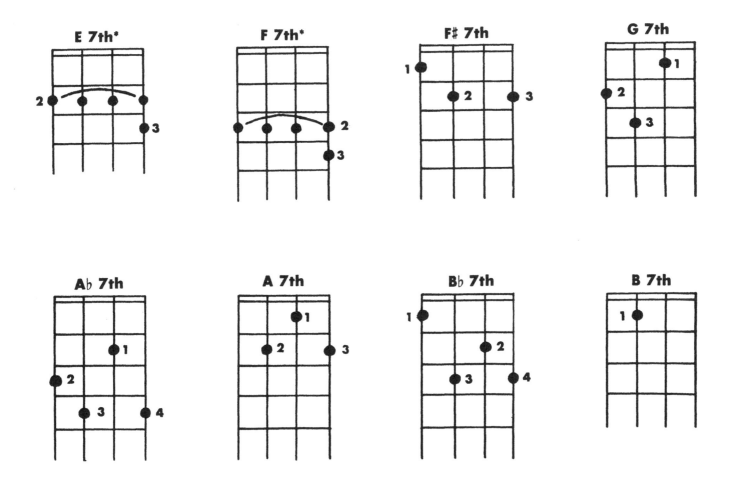

* Note: Some players find it easier to use the 1st and 2nd fingers in playing the Eb 7th, E 7th, and F 7th chords instead of the fingering indicated here. Take your choice. However, in changing from an E 7th to an A 7th chord — a common change when playing in either the key of G, or D, for example — most players find it more convenient to use the fingering shown on the diagrams above.

"CHORD TRICKS"

You don't have to be a magician to learn the "chord tricks" on this page, and those that follow! First we start with an old friend from Exercise No. 1—D 7th. Study the diagrams carefully. At first they may appear somewhat complicated; but as you study these chord patterns and take time to really work them out, you'll find the going smoother than you imagined. You'll get that "superior" feeling when you find yourself playing not just *one* D 7th chord, for example, but *FOUR* of 'em!

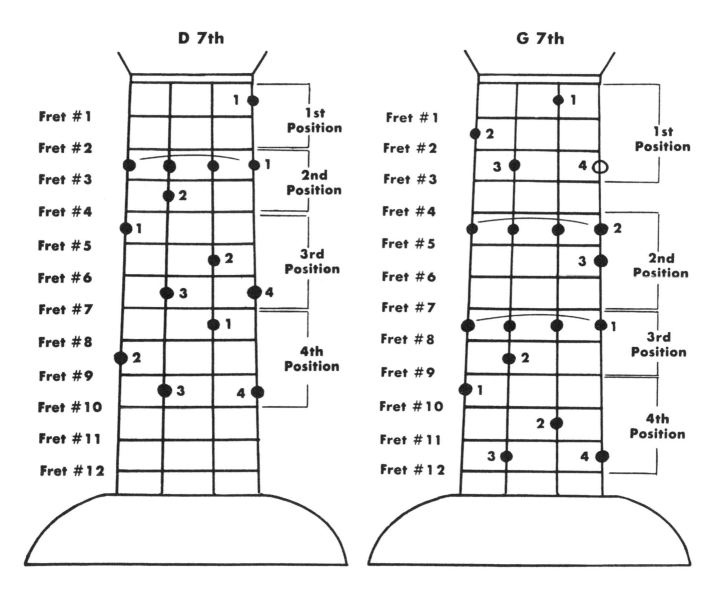

If at first you didn't succeed — try, try again! There are more of these "Chord tricks" coming up—BUT NOT ONE OF THEM WILL BE BEYOND YOUR CAPACITY *IF YOU HAVE REALLY PRACTICED THESE!* Fact is, these chord studies should become easier and more fun as you go along. And one of these days you'll be surprised to find yourself working out actual *melodies* — not just playing chord accompaniments. That's what these "chord tricks" are designed to do: Make it possible for you to learn to play melody.

"Chord Tricks"

(continued)

In this exercise, we put the A 7th and C 7th chords through their paces!

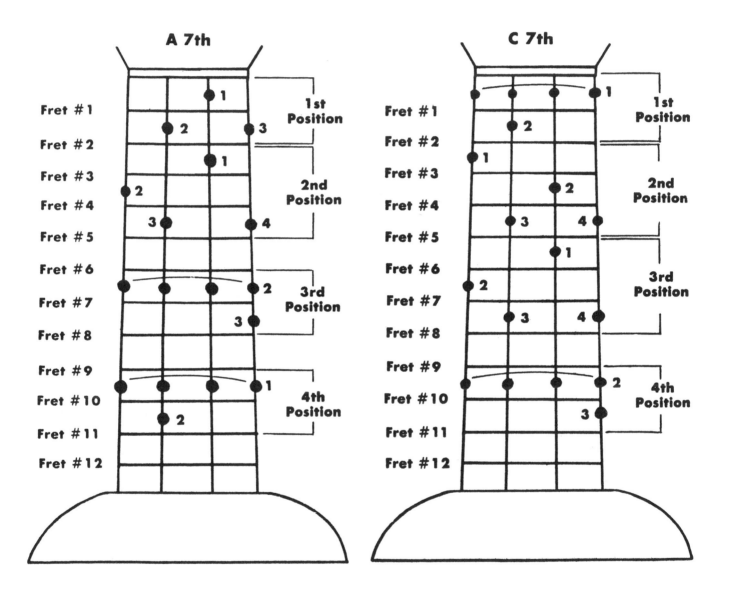

Note in the above diagrams that the *fingering* for the A 7th 3rd position and the C 7th 4th position is *identical*. Only the *location* on the fingerboard differs. The same thing is true for the fingering of the A 7th 2nd position and the C 7th 3rd position: The fingering is *identical* — only the *location* on the fingerboard differs.

"Chord Tricks"

(more of same!)

Here, two more familiar chords — B 7th and E 7th — do their stuff!

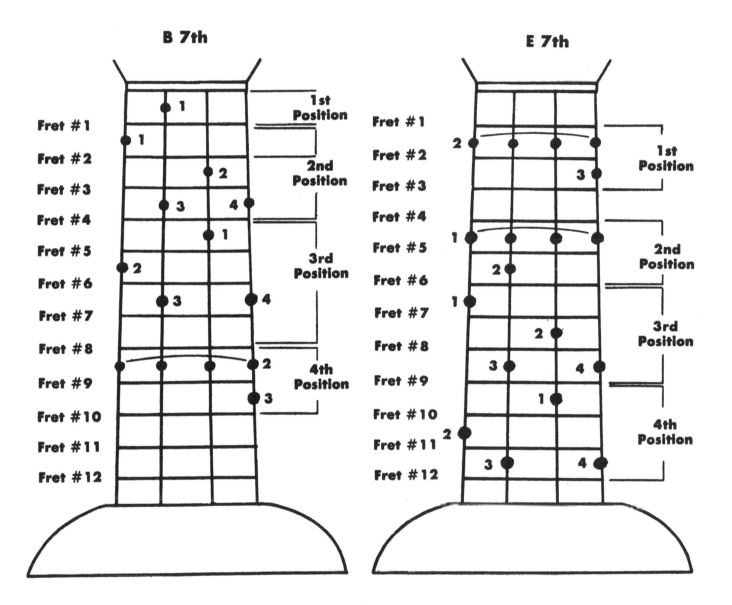

By this time you've seen how these chord progressions — all of 'em — follow a set pattern in which the same basic chord formations repeat themselves in different positions on the fingerboard. Above, for example, compare the B 7th 2nd position with the E 7th 3rd position. Now compare these to the C 7th 2nd position on previous page. The *same fingering* is used in each case — only the *location* on the fingerboard differs.

"FANCY STUFF"

Here are some additional fancy chords to pull out of the hat. You may not meet them too frequently in the average song, but they are — or should be — part of every accomplished ukulele player's repertoire.

AUGMENTED FIFTHS

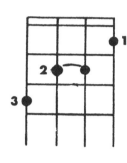 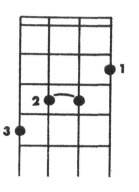 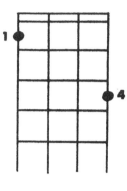 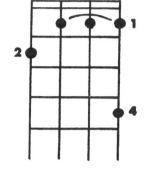

MINOR SIXTHS

| B♭ min. 6 | B min 6 | E♭ min. 6 | E min. 6 |

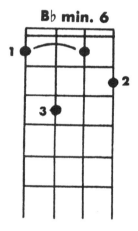 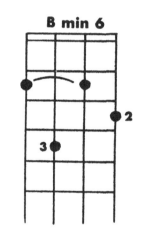 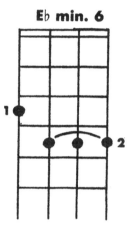 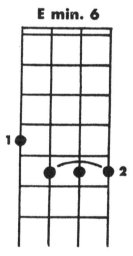

NINTH CHORDS

| C 9th | C# 9th | D 9th | E♭ 9th |

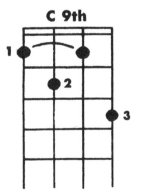 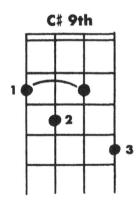 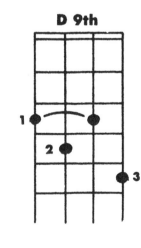 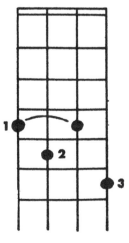

YOU CAN PLAY THE UKULELE

SONG FAVORITES

•

Index

The Streets Of Laredo

Key of C

1. As I _____ walked out in The Streets Of La -
2. "I see by your out - fit that you are a
3. It was once in the sad - dle I used to go

re - do, as _____ I _____ walked out in La - re - do one
cow - boy," these _____ words he did say as I bold - ly stepped
dash - ing, it was once in the sad - dle I used to go

day, I spied a cow - punch - er wrapped up in white
by; "Come sit down be - side me and hear my sad
gay; _____ First to the dram - house and then to the

lin - en, wrapped up in white lin - en, as cold as the clay.
sto - ry; I am shot in the breast and I know I must die."
card - house; got ___ shot in the breast and I'm dy - ing to - day.

Git Along Little Dōgies

Key of G

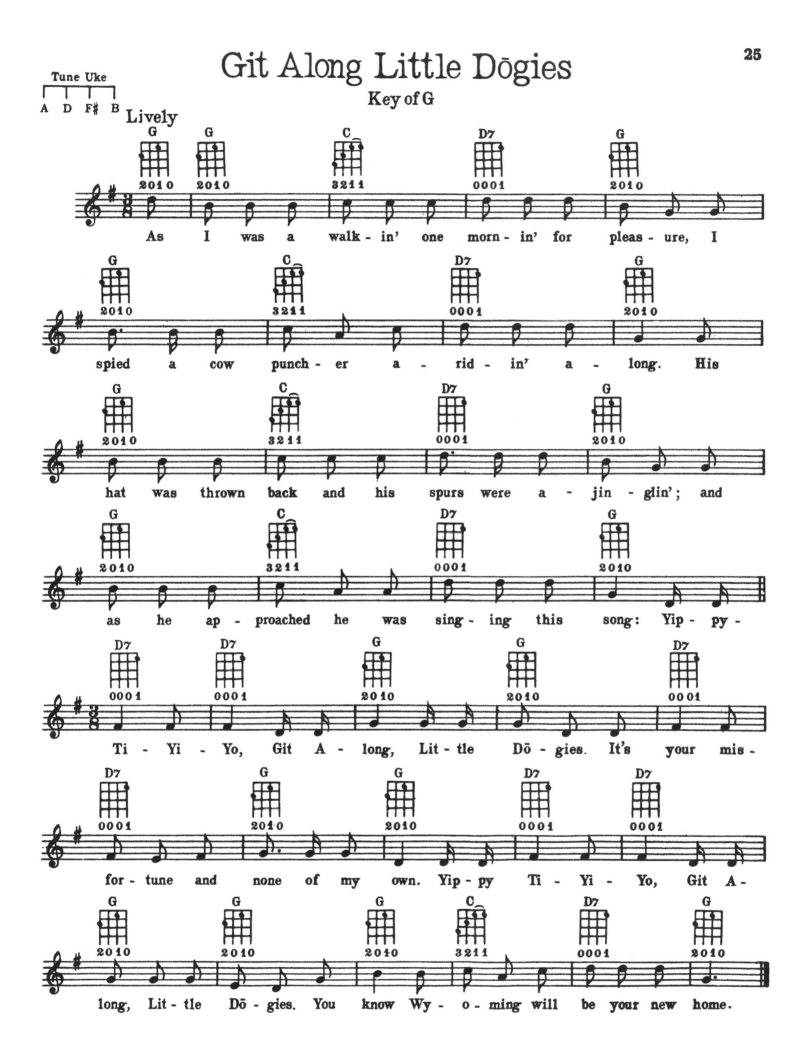

Red River Valley

Key of A

Home On The Range

Key of D

Oh! Susanna

Key of C

By STEPHEN FOSTER

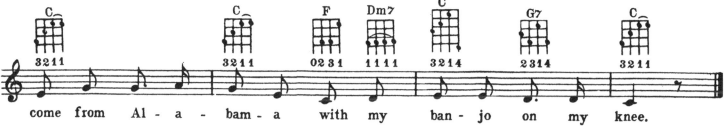

(Note: If you'd like to try your hand at a bit of melody play the last three measures of the Chorus as indicated below.)

Far Above Cayuga's Waters

Key of A

C. K. URGUHART

On, Wisconsin!

Washington And Lee Swing

Washington and Lee University
Key of C

Words and Music by
THORNTON W. ALLEN,
C. A. ROBBINS &
M. W. SHEAFE

Rambling Wreck From Georgia Tech

Georgia Institute of Technology

Key of D

The Bluetail Fly
Key of D

Slowly, with expression

1. When I was young I used to wait on
2. One day he rode a - round the farm, he
3. The po - ny run, he jump and pitch, and
4. Old Mas - sa's gone, now let him rest; they

Mas - sa and hand to him a plate, and pass the bot - tle when
did - n't take me and the flies just swarm. One chanced to bite him
throwed old Mas - sa in the ditch, he died and the ju - ry
say all things are for the best. I never for - get, till the

he got dry, and brush a - way the Blue - tail Fly.
in the eye. The dev - il take that Blue - tail Fly.
won - dered why; the rea - son was the Blue - tail Fly.
day I die, old Mas - sa and that Blue - tail Fly.

Faster

Jim - my crack corn, and I don't care, Jim - my crack corn, and I don't care,

Jim - my crack corn, and I don't care, old Mas - sa's gone a - way.

Foggy, Foggy Dew

Key of G

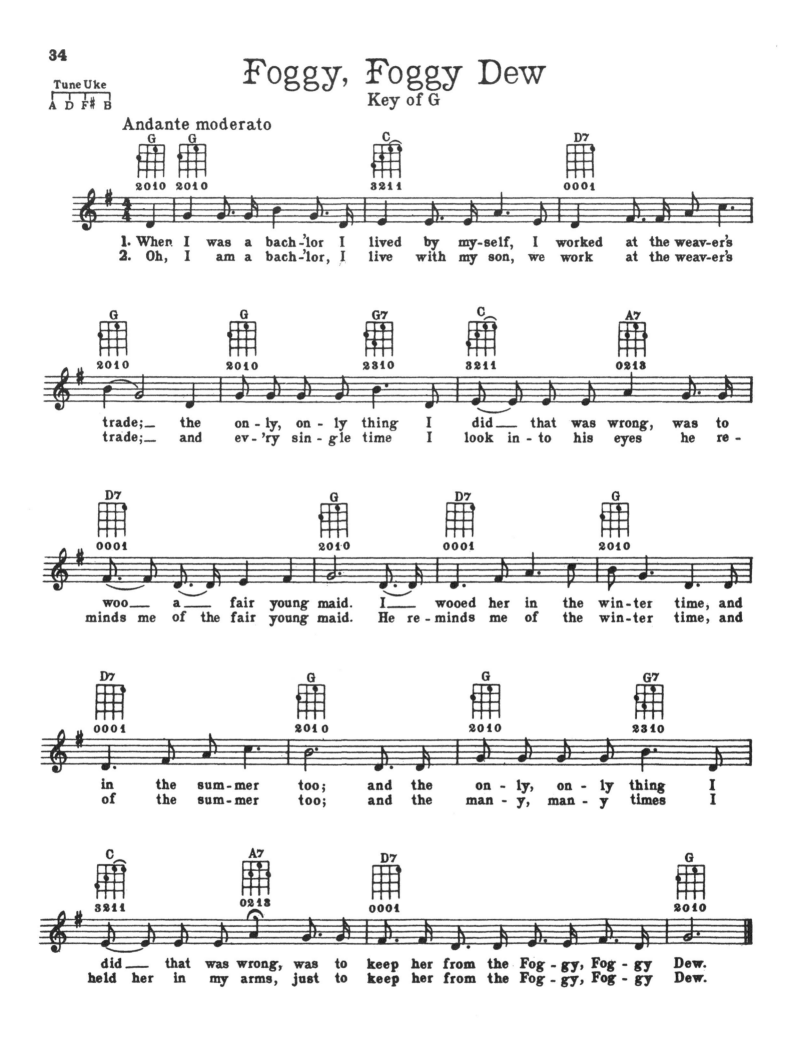

She'll Be Comin' 'Round The Mountain

Key of G

Tune Uke
A D F♯ B

Brightly

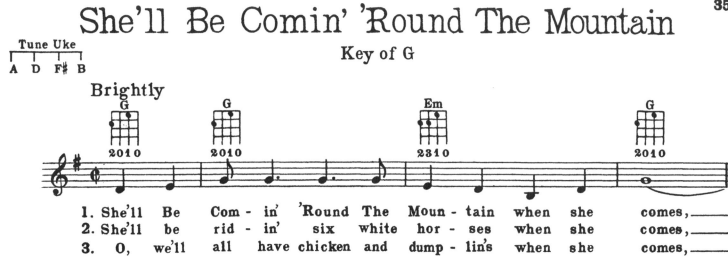

1. She'll Be Com - in' 'Round The Moun - tain when she comes,___
2. She'll be rid - in' six white hor - ses when she comes,___
3. O, we'll all have chicken and dump - lin's when she comes,___

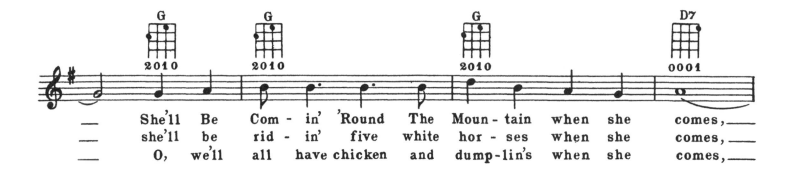

___ She'll Be Com - in' 'Round The Moun - tain when she comes,___
___ she'll be rid - in' five white hor - ses when she comes,___
___ O, we'll all have chicken and dump - lin's when she comes,___

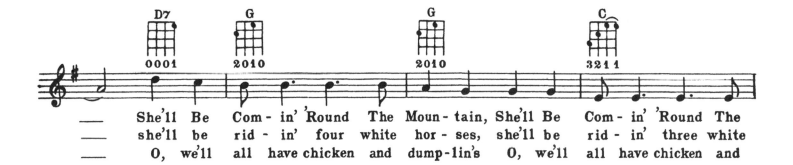

___ She'll Be Com - in' 'Round The Moun - tain, She'll Be Com - in' 'Round The
___ she'll be rid - in' four white hor - ses, she'll be rid - in' three white
___ O, we'll all have chicken and dump - lin's O, we'll all have chicken and

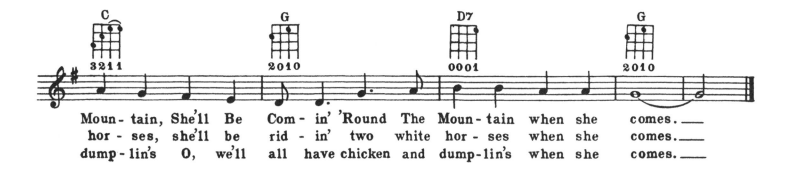

Moun - tain, She'll Be Com - in' 'Round The Moun - tain when she comes.___
hor - ses, she'll be rid - in' two white hor - ses when she comes.___
dump - lin's O, we'll all have chicken and dump-lin's when she comes.___

Betsy From Pike
Key of C

Tune Uke
A D F♯ B

Moderato

1. Oh, don't you re - mem - ber sweet Bet - sy From Pike, who
2. The roos - ter ran off and the cat - tle all died, and
3. One morn - ing they climbed to the top of a hill, and

crossed the big moun - tains with her lov - er Ike, with two yoke of
fin - 'ly the last piece of her ba - con was fried. Poor Ike got dis -
saw e - nough gold all their pock - ets to fill. Ike shout - ed and

cat - tle and a large yel - low dog, a __ tall Shang - hai roos - ter and
cour - aged and Bet - sy got mad; the __ dog wagged his tail and looked
said, as he sat in the shade, "Sweet Bet - sy, my dar - ling, our

one spot - ted hog? Say - ing, "Good - bye, Pike Coun - ty, fare - well for a
woe - ful - ly sad. Sing - ing, "Too - ra - la too - ra - la too - ra - la -
for - tune is made!" Say - ing, "Good - bye, Pike Coun - ty, fare - well for a

while. We'll __ come back a - gain when we've panned out our pile."
loo," sing-ing, "Too - ra - la, too - ra - la, boo - hoo - hoo - hoo."
while. We'll __ come back a - gain when we've panned out our pile."

In The Evening By The Moonlight

Key of D

JAMES BLAND

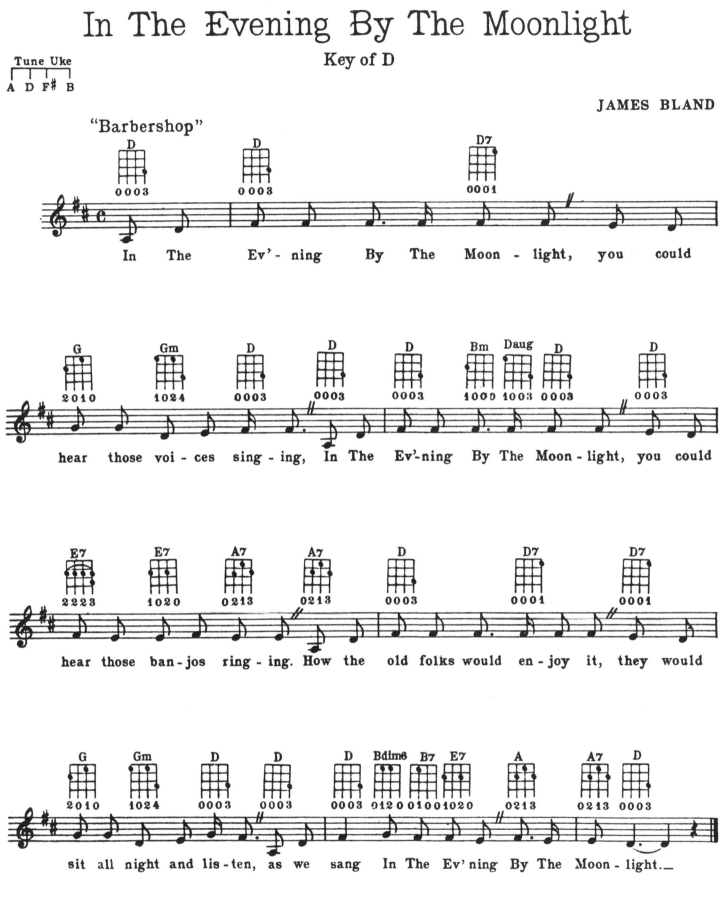

Sweet And Low

Key of A

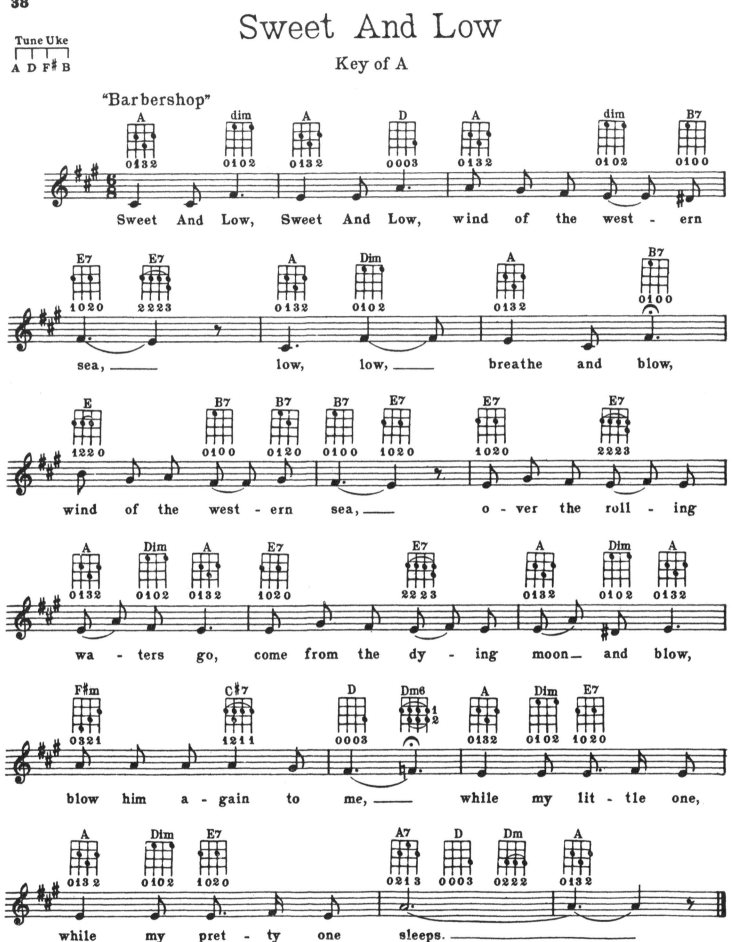

You Tell Me Your Dream

Key of G

By S. RICE
A. H. BROWN
C. DANIELS

Tune Uke
A D F♯ B

"Barbershop"

I Had A Dream Dear, you had one

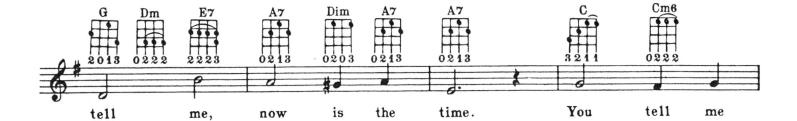

too. Mine was the best dream be -

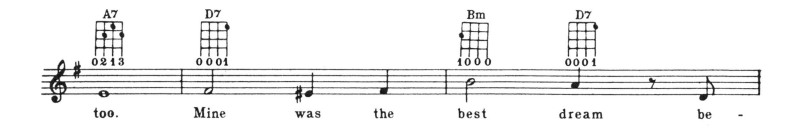

cause it was of you. Come, sweet - heart

tell me, now is the time. You tell me

your dream and I will tell you mine.

Whispering Hope
Key of C

ALICE HAWTHORNE

1. Soft as the voice of an An - gel, breath-ing a les-son un - heard,—
2. If, in the dusk of the twi - light, dim be the re-gion a - far,—

Hope, with a gen-tle per-sua - sion, whis pers her com-fort-ing word.—
will not the deep-en-ing dark - ness bright-en the glim-mer-ing star?—

Wait till the dark-ness is o - ver, wait till the tem-pest is done,—
Then, when the night is up - on us, why should the heart sink a - way?—

hope for the sun-shine to-mor - row, af - ter the show - er is gone.—
When the dark mid-night is o - ver, watch for the break-ing of day.—

Whis-per-ing, Whis-per-ing Hope,— oh, how wel-come Thy voice, oh, how wel - come,

mak - ing my heart in its sor - row re - joice,— re - joice!—